LAURA K. MURRAY

ANGELS

ARE THEY REAL?

CREATIVE EDUCATION · CREATIVE PAPERBACKS

Published by Creative Education and Creative Paperbacks
P.O. Box 227, Mankato, Minnesota 56002
Creative Education and Creative Paperbacks are imprints of The Creative Company
www.thecreativecompany.us

Design and production by **Christine Vanderbeek**
Art direction by **Rita Marshall**
Printed in the United States of America

Photographs by Corbis (Corbis, Robert Marien, Summerfield Press), Creative Commons Wikimedia (Vladimir Borovikovsky/icon-art. info, Vladimir Borovikovsky/State Russian Museum, Raphael/Louvre Museum, Abbott Handerson Thayer/Smithsonian American Art Museum/Gift of John Gellatly), Dreamstime (Cadmancan, Lane Erickson, Kmiragaya, Janusz Kwiatkowski, Mentona, Duncan Noakes, Andriy Petrenko, Jozef Sedmak, Starblue, Sudok1, Petrov Yevgeniy), iStockphoto (Fitzer, ZvonimirAtleti), Shutterstock (chanus, Dragan85)

Library of Congress Cataloging-in-Publication Data
Murray, Laura K.   Angels / Laura K. Murray.   p. cm. – (Are they real?)   Includes index.   Summary: A high-interest inquiry into the possible existence of angels, emphasizing reported sightings and stories as well as studies, polls, and religious accounts.
ISBN 978-1-60818-760-7 (hardcover)   **ISBN 978-1-62832-368-9** (pbk)   **ISBN 978-1-56660-802-2** (ebook)
1. Angels–Juvenile literature.
BL477.M87 2017
202/.15–dc23   2016008266

CCSS: RI.1.1, 2, 4, 5, 6, 7, 10; RI.2.1, 2, 4, 5, 6, 7; RI.3.1, 2, 5, 6, 7; RF.1.1, 2, 3, 4; RF.2.3, 4; RF.3.3, 4

First Edition HC 9 8 7 6 5 4 3 2 1   **First Edition PBK** 9 8 7 6 5 4 3 2 1

CONTENTS

A VOICE

Firefighter Ty Jodouin is alone inside a burning building. His air tank stops working. Ty cannot see through the smoke. What is that clear voice?

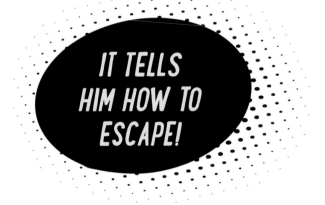

IT TELLS HIM HOW TO ESCAPE!

SPIRIT MESSENGERS

Angels are spirits that do good work. Some **RELIGIONS** teach that angels bring messages from God.

People may think of angels as loved ones who have died. But **SKEPTICS** do not believe angels are real.

WHAT DO ANGELS LOOK LIKE?

People often picture angels as beings with wings.

They may wear white robes and have **HALOS**. But maybe angels look like beautiful lights. Or maybe you can't see them at all!

WHAT DO ANGELS DO?

Angels can bring comfort or healing. Guardian angels are said to watch over humans.

Other angels might be warriors. They fight evil. Sometimes angels talk to people in dreams.

Some people study angels. Others collect stories from **WITNESSES**. Skeptics explain angels as being kind strangers. Or maybe they are simply tricks of the light.

12

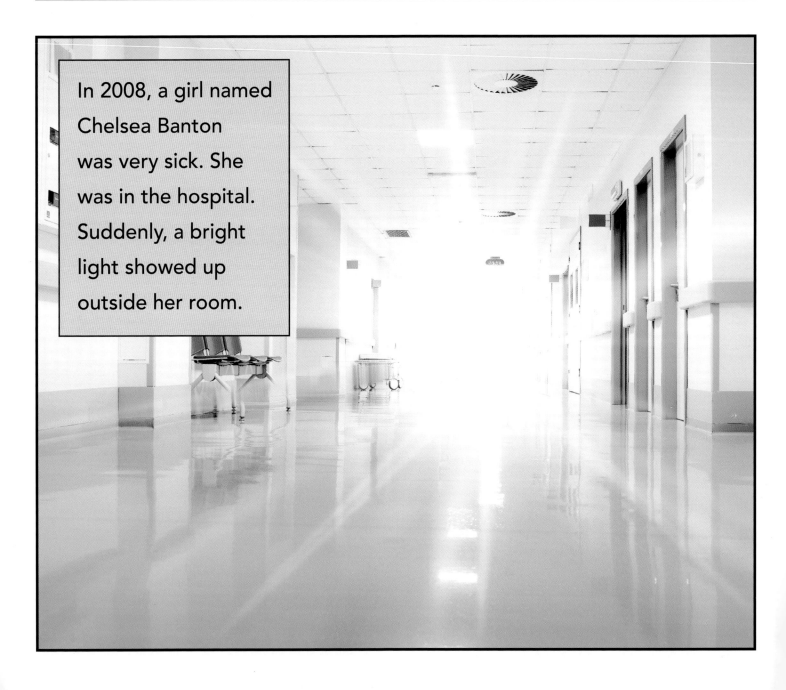

In 2008, a girl named Chelsea Banton was very sick. She was in the hospital. Suddenly, a bright light showed up outside her room.

Then she got better!
Chelsea's mom and
nurses thought the
light was an angel.

FROM DA VINCI'S ANNUNCIATION

People put angels in songs, movies, and poems. Painters
like Leonardo da Vinci imagined what angels are like.

Angels in art often play instruments.
Sometimes they look like children.

ANGEL ENCOUNTERS

POLLS have found that most Americans believe in angels. People may not agree about angels. But they will keep listening and watching.

What would you do if you saw an angel?

LISTEN FOR THE FLUTTER OF WINGS!

INVESTIGATE IT!
ANGEL POLL

Take a poll of your family and friends. Ask if they believe in angels. Have they ever seen or heard one? Record their answers in a notebook. Then look at your results. Do the answers surprise you? What other questions do you have?

DO YOU BELIEVE IN ANGELS?

YES
IIII

NO
II

22

GLOSSARY

HALOS circles of light

POLLS the asking of the same question to different people

RELIGIONS beliefs in God or gods

SKEPTICS people who question a belief

WITNESSES people who see an event

READ MORE

Harris, Annaka. *I Wonder*. Calif.: Four Elephants, 2013.

What Do You Believe? New York: DK, 2011.

WEBSITES

Angel Coloring Pages
http://www.coloring.ws/angels.htm
Find a picture of an angel to print and color.

The Louvre: Angel Artwork
http://www.louvre.fr/en/moteur-de-recherche-oeuvres
Search for "Angels" to see artwork at France's Louvre Museum.

Note: Every effort has been made to ensure that the websites listed above are suitable for children, that they have educational value, and that they contain no inappropriate material. However, because of the nature of the Internet, it is impossible to guarantee that these sites will remain active indefinitely or that their contents will not be altered.

INDEX